Things Worth
Seeing

Produced by Duncan McCorquodale.
Designed by Christian Küsters
with the contribution of Philippa Walz.
Copy edited by Maria Wilson.

Printed in the European Union.

ISBN 1 901033 26 0

British Library cataloguing-in-publication data.
A catalogue record of this book is available from
The British Library.

for Sabine

Things Worth
Seeing

A guide to the city of W

William Firebrace

The city of W lies beside the river Dibo, at the point where the mountains join the plains.

Among the various nationalities populating the city are: Hungarians, Czecks, Tyrolians, Carinthians, Mexicans, Croatians, Slovaks, Bosnians, Slovenes, Poles, Lombards, Styrians, Austrians, Serbs, Jews, Saxons, Ashanti, Transylvanians, Ruthenians, Ukranians, Galicians, Armenians and Wallachians.

The city is known by various names, the most commonly used being Weiden or Wieden, Vins or Mecs, Wina or Vrina.

W
Things Worth Seeing

1. Altstadt Friseur
2. Antonstadt Maria and Elizabetta Church
3. Landweg Palais Minutti
4. Luisedorf Flak Towers
5. Siglavy Natural History Museum
6. Neubach Opera House
7. Himmelstadt Museum Riedolfski
8. Kalksburg City Library
9. Jedlesee Riding School
10. Ost-Kopping Botanical Garden
11. Webbing House Chaink
12. Brummering Hospital
13. Speising Monument to the Heroes
14. Malzing Woods
15. Theresastadt Höbbelsalon
16. Conversano Museum des Unglaubens
17. Krebling Haus Reiner
18. Rosenau Konditorei
19. Mariagrund Railway Station
20. Möhning-Steindorf Men's Outfitters
21. Limming Bathing Resort
22. Morgenstadt Great Wheel
23. Zernals Tram Stop

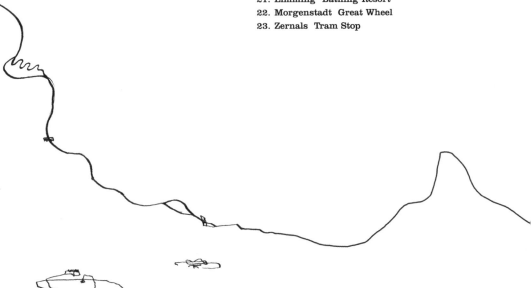

Things Worth Seeing

On a flight to a north European city, as the plane is coming
in to land and as a slight fog drifts over the aircraft wing,
I hear the voice of the stewardess, speaking in German, her
accent very pronounced so that the vowels sound rather high
with emphasis on the i's and e's, and I suddenly recall the city
of W, where the inhabitants speak with a similar dialect, and
where my family lived during certain years of my childhood,
while I alone remained behind in a school in our home
country, to be correctly educated. In this school, where the
corridors seem to be filled with the noise of animals fighting,
the other children often amuse themselves by calling me a
Nazi, and although I don't know what Nazis are, and consider
the word only a mispronunciation of the word nasty, it
seems at least individual to be a Nazi, I feel a certain pride.
Occasionally, after long months of study, a message comes
with the news that it is time for me to visit W. I journey
alone, with my own passport, into which is pasted my photo,
wearing my smartest clothes and travelling by aeroplane,
it is important to travel by aeroplane, where there are no
other children, the other children cannot come, and where
the sound of the engines allows no silence. The stewardess
straps me in with a canvas belt and brings the food on
a special tray with holes for each item. Nobody asks
me to recite the names of rivers or to spell long words.
There appear to be no punishments, I hope there are no
punishments, sometimes it is difficult to know when there

may not be a sudden unforeseen test followed almost always
by a punishment. At the airport barrier await my parents,
I must be attentive and recognise them and not choose the
wrong parents. There they are, wearing long green coats
of a felt like material, and carrying a small brown dog,
I recognise the dog, it is really the clue, without the dog it
would be difficult to certain. Now I must remember how to
behave with them, they will ask me questions, I must give
the right answers, the same answers as last time, I must try
to remember which answers I gave last time. We live in a
flat on the third floor, the stairs wind round and round, the
steps are made of stone and once a man slipped here and fell,
he broke his leg or perhaps his arm, I imagine him wearing
a grey suit and a small green hat with a feather, his body
folded into a ball slowly tumbling down, over and over, turning
carefully at the landings, but I must hold on to the rail and
be careful not to fall, and also to make no noise on the stairs,
the people in the other flats will be angry, their anger must
be avoided, it is better when no one is angry. Inside our flat
I look carefully to see if anything has changed, the tables
and upright chairs seem to be in the same position, and the
pictures on the wall seem the same, the women still dancing,
the carriages still arriving, the soldiers still marching, the
small spidery foreign writing still unreadable. There are
scratches on the dining room table, white scars, I can run
my finger in them and feel the roughness of the wood, my
mother says however hard she polishes they will never come
out, a visitor, that Hungarian man, a real terror, must have
made them, cracking nuts, he won't be invited here again,
even if he comes to the door, even if he calls his name and
waits, he will be told to go away. It's already time to go, we
can't stay inside all day, we must do things, we will visit
the sights, see the things that are important, walking through
the city is a special treat. We walk together past grand
buildings with no roofs, their windows without glass, the

walls fenced off with timber barriers. Crude letters painted
on wooden posts tell us which building is which. Sometimes
there are soldiers outside with rifles, they look like our soldiers
but they are not our soldiers, so we must not talk to them,
we may tell them something they must not know. It is windy,
I think I don't like it here, it's so untidy. Why doesn't somebody
tidy everything up? Why are there so many stones in the road,
making it difficult for the cars? A man say's it wasn't the
English that bombed the city, it couldn't be the English, they
are always our friends, perhaps it was the Americans, they
are different, or the Russians, the Russians are very bad
people, we must never talk to the Russians, they steal children,
and never bring them back, the Russians must have done
this thing. I hear my father speaking to people in words I
don't understand, he even speaks to the Russians in their
own language, but he never speaks to us in anything but
English. I wish I could speak to the Germans and to the
Russians, and to their children, but the other children can't
speak any English, so we move our arms in circles and use
signs, we sometimes understand each other. My father records
the monuments of the city with his camera. We wait in line,
looking towards him, as he studies a small light meter in a
leather case, repeating the numbers out loud, 1.8, 2.8, 4, 5.6,
11, 16, wonderful expanding sequence of numbers, which
I repeat silently to myself, the numbers and the light, only
these and no more, we want to go, why does it take so long,
stand still, baby stop crying, all smile, please smile, the timer
begins to whirr, quick, father runs to get in the picture.
Sometimes he goes away, to another city, perhaps to Russia,
he never tells us where he goes, or why we live here away
from our own land, no-one can ask him, no-one even thinks
to ask. He loves numbers and sits in a small armchair filling
sheets of squared paper with lists of figures, writing carefully
in ballpoint so that the figures fit into the squares, working
out some complex problem. We must be quiet and then all

the figures will work out, if only all the numbers will add up. My mother plays records of operettas, my father plants the hyacinth bulbs in glass bowls filled to the neck with water. My mother conceals them in cupboards, on the top shelf in the darkness, I want to see them and smell their strong perfume. Not yet, you must wait until spring, if you open the door the light will come in and then there will be no flowers. In the bookshelf in the dining room there is a book, with a long title, too long to be read, all in Gothic script. The book is too big for the shelf, so it has to lie sideways, projecting awkwardly. I take the book out of the shelf and lie on the floor of the living room, turning over the pages with the photographs of the Opera House, and the Cathedral and the Palace of the Emperor, all whole and not destroyed, difficult to match with those piles of stones I see in the city, the pictures filled with people in old fashioned clothing, no soldiers with rifles. Beside the pages are lists of figures and names, sizes and dates, comforting to decipher and read out loud. One evening, as we drive through the streets, my father says we will leave W, the dog barks, never come back, he says we are going to live in another city, beside the sea, but it doesn't matter to me, I don't live here anyway, and I have never heard of this other city. I sit in the back of the car and see a factory with bright neon lights, hanging high in the sky, illuminating pieces of wall and pipes. One city is much like another. The trams here in W are coloured red and yellow and green according to which of the various routes they belong to, tickets can be purchased in booklets of ten from tobacconists or from the major rail stations. There is nothing much to pack.

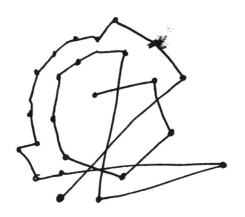

A Visit

A business trip. Autumn of 1992. I visit W again. The city
seems clean, dull, touristic. In a coffee house beside the
market well-dressed men and women sit reading newspapers,
the pages a curious sky blue. The waiter comes, carrying
a small glass of water on a metal tray. Also, please, some
noodles, yes like the man in the corner is eating. They aren't
noodles? So, very different, made of egg and cheese, with
some herbs, yes, then those please. I try to recall the time
my family lived in W but can summon up only images that
seem artificial, images seen as though from outside. While
finishing the dish that resembles noodles, I realise that I
have some considerable time to spare. I examine the city map,
with its complex folding system, and find at the back a list
of Sehenswürdigkeiten, a description in alphabetical order of
the city sights. There are 23 city districts, each with a name
and number. I imagine an itinerary, visiting one sight in
each of the city districts, beginning at the centre in the First
District, Altstadt, winding through the districts of the inner
and outer rings and ending in the Twenty-third, Zernals,
on the edge of the woods. I consider how long it would take
to complete such an itinerary, and how complicated it would
be to move from one point to another. On a napkin I draw a
sketch of the route, numbering the points, a line spiralling
around on itself, with irregular backward movements and
sudden jumps across the spiral. The ink sinks into the napkin
and blotches at the points.

1

Friseur

Walter-Schnalk-Gasse 8
Altstadt

The Altstadt, corresponding to the mediaeval city, was once surrounded by the city wall with eight gates. The narrow streets of this area wind between the locations of the gates. Many of the streets take the form of dead-ends or U's, making movement in a straight line difficult.
Certain streets were once assigned to specific trades –
Hans-Josef-Gasse: milliners.
Arnold-Maitsch-Gasse: nail makers.
Ernalsstraße: enamel and silver workers.
Solto-Gasse: vendors of offal.
In the early nineteenth-century the encircling wall was removed and replaced by a wide avenue lined with trees. At this time several wide straight avenues were cut through the dense structure of the Altstadt. Walter-Schnalk-Gasse 8, now occupied by a barber's shop, was formerly the house of the long distance runner Heini Goloni, who gained two Gold Medals in the 1932 Olympic Games, and who later originated the Goloni technique, involving a rigorous diet for amateur sports training.

A room with two stools and a long wooden bench, covered in red leather.

On the radio the sound of a football game, with an excited
commentator. Interruption for commercial.

The buzzing of the shears. I sit and wait. Start off with
a haircut.

Over-inquisitive children peering through the window.

Anton Lipp. Barber. Master Diploma from Grentz Academy
of Personal Appearance 1958.

His hand on the back of my neck. Slight pressure.

BARBER Just bend forward a little, put your head in the bowl,
a little deeper, it's not too cold, or too warm maybe, yes now
don't be afraid, the water is not so deep that any harm can
come, don't breathe in through your nose, or also not through
your mouth, particularly not through your mouth, now open
your eyes, the water won't harm you, it's very clean, pure
water, from the hills, what can you see now? no please don't
try to answer, the question was only just a way of speaking,
no answer is needed at all, yes, you never saw such things
before, the surface of the bowl, white, very white, and all those
little scratches on the enamel, they seem very clear now that
you see them so close, I'm not holding you too tight am I?
again no answer is necessary, just a movement of the
shoulders, there, a little deeper and it won't take long, that
seems more comfortable, look now at the pattern of the
scratches and the way the water seems to make them clearer,
and how the little bubbles of air seem to gather along the lines
of the scratches, where the black of the metal is visible, the
bubbles don't seem to move, but they always seem to be on
the point of moving, always on the point of drifting away
upwards, but never actually moving, never even growing in
size, it must be something to do with the chemistry between

the metal and the enamel and the water, the one against the
other, did they move? did they move then? easy, easy now,
probably they only seemed as if they moved, no, I myself, I
never travel much, it seems enough to wait for people to come
here, yes into the countryside of course, in the summertime,
well really only out to the edge of the city, where the houses
stop and the trees and fields begin, one can't really call it
countryside there, but never further, it probably wouldn't
be any different if I went further, just more trees and more
fields, and then another town, much like this one most
probably, not long now, is it warm enough?

Gentle voice. Relax now.

Let your shirt dry off.

Such stripes.

The colour of the towel.

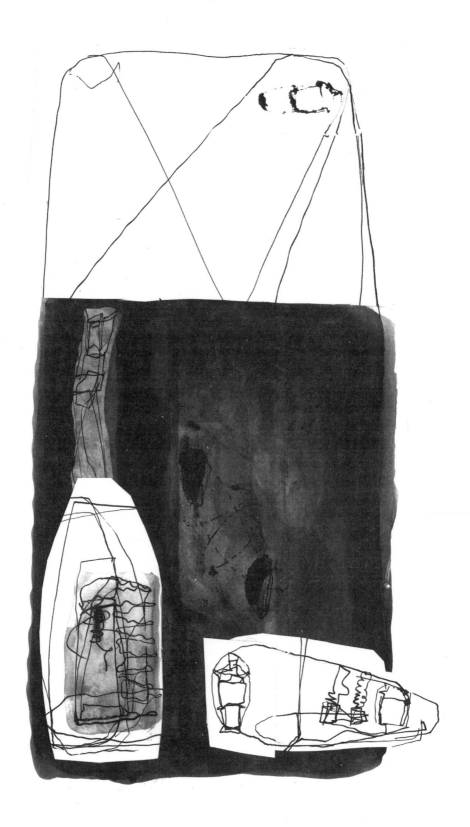

2

Maria und Elizabetta Kirche

Sauchgasse 3
Antonstadt

The exterior form of the Maria und Elizabetta Kirche
can barely be distinguished from the surrounding buildings,
but its porch with the gold coloured statues is easily located.
Original founder: Fürst Jakob, brother of the Emperor Justus,
and a believer in a return to a simpler faith.
Date of original structure: 1120–1130.
First architect: Martin the Doubter, Irish monk.
Height of nave: 26 metres.
Among the features of interest are –
Last Judgement Ceiling, 1582, commenced by
Luigi Mistioni and completed by his son Giovanni Mistioni,
with complex perspectival devices, giving the impression
of a space much larger than actually exists.
Hellman Chapel devoted to the child saint Trudi Hellman,
who is reputed to have seen a vision of a white lady beside
the river at Ubbs. This vision was followed by a series of
miraculous cures, connected to a stone found in the river.
Trudi Hellman died at the age of 22, still living in the
family home. The present location of the stone is uncertain.

Tired in the sunlight. The light is too bright. A woman says:
it is not I that you seek, but another. Look now among the
stones on the river bank. The cool of the water, the slippery
surface of the stones. Finding the right one.

A black spot in the nave of the church. A man and a woman, of North African appearance, both wearing sombre leather jackets and dark glasses stand beside me, so that we form a triangle around the black spot. Looking down we might see our feet pointing inwards towards the spot, a pair of black brogues, a pair of yellow sandals with bronze buckles, a pair of brown casuals. Looking up, our mouths slightly apart, we stare into a space that stretches above us, out of the solidity of the surrounding stones, ending in a large rectangular void through which the blue sky is visible. Clouds billow out, various angels and saints float past, reaching up to the centre of the sky. There seems to be no joint between the actual structure and the paintwork, the whole acts as one space, at the base of which are positioned our three pairs of feet, at the apex of which is a great eye, hovering in the sky, staring unblinkingly down at us. Tired of the effort of standing together, we move apart and the perspective effect begins to collapse, the roof appears to slip, the floating figures become distorted, stretching out into unrecognisable elongated forms, as though the unstable vision were only held together by the triangle of viewers.

Alone in a smaller unlit space, to the side of the building.

A clear glass window shows the figure of a girl standing beside a river. Behind the girl there is a glow of light. The window is just above eye-level, so that the viewer looks up and through it. The girl holds in her hand a stone, inscribed with an oval groove.

Sickly eyes raised.
Dim angelic gaze.
Water dripping from her hand.

Some young women come past, dressed in pink and green
cycling suits. The green almost matches the green of the
marble on the columns, so that the women appear curiously
camouflaged. They whisper loudly. He came round last
night. No, really. Yes, he came round and this time he stayed.
And? Wait.

Before the window is a small metal stand with candles
burning. I look at the flames, but they are diffused, it is
impossible to concentrate on any one. For one moment
I am tempted to light a candle. I think, if I light a candle
then something will be revealed. If not now, then later.
If I don't light the candle the chance will be missed, more
than missed because I considered lighting the candle
and then didn't. I hesitate, ashamed of my superstition.
I reach in my pocket for a coin. I run my finger around
the groove in the coin, I feel the moisture from my finger
against the smoothness of the metal.

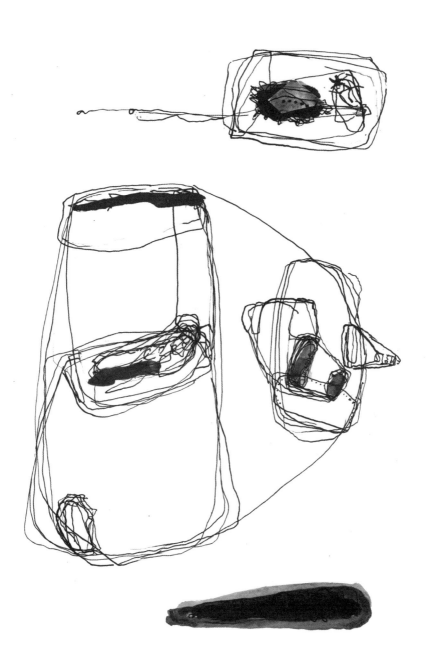

3

Palais Minutti

Zipstraße 46
Landweg

The Palais Minutti lies at the junction of Zipstraße and
Wermundstraße. Its long pink facade stands out amongst
the surrounding grey buildings.
Architects: the Hungarian brothers János and György Koláks.
Length of street facade: 128 metres.
Number of columns: 75.
Completion date: 1834.
Number of rooms: 127, including the Scarlet Chamber, once the
bedroom of Maria Minutti, known as the Fake Empress. Maria
Minutti came from humble origins, but married into the wealthy
Minutti family, whose fortune was based on iron smelting and
the casting of cannons. She held a court considered by some to be
more magnificent than that of the imperial family, but vanished
in mysterious circumstances, while travelling by coach in the
mountains, in the winter of 1842. Neither her body, nor that of
her four year old child Elena, who was travelling with her, were
ever discovered. The palace was badly damaged in the war years
and only partially rebuilt.

Above the words is a small drawing, possibly anatomical,
possibly a landscape with a river and some stunted trees.

On the wall is written:
I LOVE SONJA AND HATE HER ON FRIDAYS BETWEEN
16.00 AND 18.00.

A few steps beyond, beside the doorway, three lines are
inscribed in blunt pencil:

THE INDIVISIBILITY OF NUMBERS.
THE WHORES OF GREECE.
THE DISEASE IS SPREADING.

Why do you look so angry?

Inside the doorway, a stair leads up to the first floor and a
narrow corridor. At the window stand a man and a woman,
arguing softly but fiercely.

You are always so angry.
Of course, of course.
You don't know what you want with me.
You don't know anything.

A small child, forgotten by the adults, and dressed in a yellow
crawlsuit, stands by a plinth on which is mounted a vase.
The child reaches up to the vase with its arms outstretched,
one of the women looks down abstractedly. The vase wobbles
on its stand.

I move uncertainly. To walk past them seems to mean
becoming involved in the argument. They glance at me but
pay no attention.

You don't speak to me any more.
You never touch me.
Don't, don't, now is not the right time.

Don't you want me any more?
Watch out, watch out, the vase, it's falling.

I push open a door and step into a large room filled with
sunlight. The room has eight sides, two with windows, two
with doors, four plain, each wall is painted a pure scarlet,
so that the room glows with a powerful internal light. The
paint does not quite reach the edges of the walls, so that an
area of raw, pinkish plaster shows through, giving the walls
the appearance of panels. The colours radiate in the room,
pushing the walls out away from each other. At the side of
the room stands a bed with four posts carved in wood, painted
a deep red. I close my eyes against the light, but I still see
against my eyelids, the outlines of the windows, lit up in
a fluorescent green, surrounded by a soft robin's-egg blue.

A short corridor leads into a second room, which seems
half-lit. The colours of the after-image still flare across
my eyes. The walls of this room are painted with stencilled
patterns. The window looks out onto a small sunlit court.
Beside one wall I make out what seems at first to be a couch,
but I realise that it is a small coach, with wooden wheels,
a shaft of wood, a seat upholstered in grey material. The
device is constructed to a miniature scale as though to be
drawn by large dogs. A complicated folding step hangs
beneath the door.

I kneel down to look into the interior. On the door is painted
the naked figure of a youth, rays of sunlight spread out above
his head, raising his hands as though in greeting.

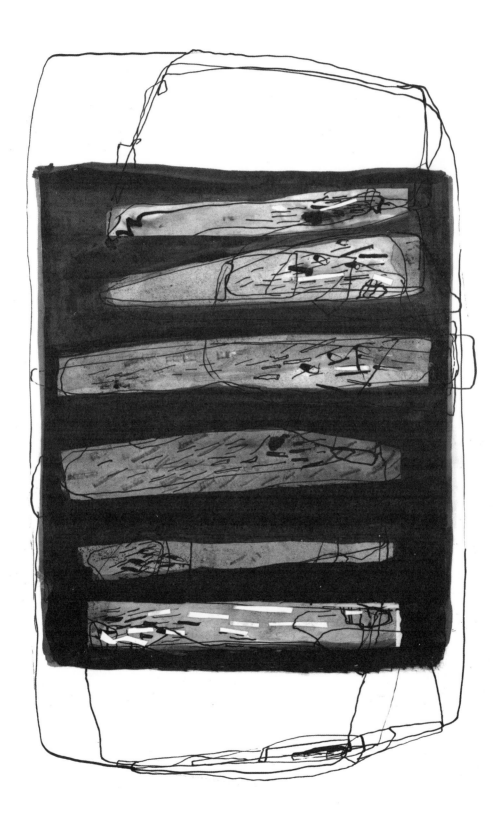

4

The Flak Towers

Lichtenstein-Weg
Luisedorf

*In W there are six Flak Towers, arranged in three pairs to form
a triangle around the inner city. The forms of the towers consist
of square and hexagonal, square and octagonal, round and
pentagonal. The two flak towers in the Lichtenstein-Weg stand
in a small park, surrounded by chestnut and gingko trees.
Number of floors: 11.
Accommodation: Shelter for 2,300 people at the lower levels,
ammunition stores at the higher levels.
Roof: anti-aircraft cannons and searchlights.
Thickness of walls: 5 metres.
The towers were constructed from reinforced concrete,
based on the military bunkers of the Eastern Front.*

Two slices of bread neatly buttered and covered with a layer
of chopped chives. A glass of cola.

The fresh green of the chives stands out sharply against the white of the plate. Each slice is cut into strips.

A hedge surrounds a small area occupied by twin rows of tables. At one side stands a small classical building hardly larger than a hut, used as a café. The only other customers are a young mother with a small girl. Behind the café stand the two grey flak towers, one octagonal, the other square, both partly covered in ivy.

A middle-aged man, dressed in a black suit, comes down between the tables, swinging his walking-stick from side to side.

MIDDLE AGED MAN More room more room.

He beats the legs of the tables. Alarmed, I move my legs carefully within the protection of my table. He sits down beside me, though the other tables around are unoccupied. At first he pays no attention to my presence, then he looks at me, rather mournfully.

MIDDLE AGED MAN There is never enough room.

SELF But there seems to be plenty of room. We are almost alone.

The man looks around, as though to check out the truth of my statement. I wish he would go, I would like to be left in peace to drink my cola. I am not sure whether this man is rather deranged, or whether he is an official with some bureaucratic purpose.

MIDDLE AGED MAN Are you a student?

SELF No, I'm just a visitor. I came to see the towers.

MIDDLE AGED MAN The towers? Don't you know there is no room in the towers? They are just lumps of concrete, what interest is there in lumps of concrete?

SELF I thought there was space inside for people to shelter during the raids.

MIDDLE AGED MAN Perhaps there was once space, perhaps there were once people inside, but now there is no space. They are solid.

SELF How do you know they are solid?

MIDDLE AGED MAN Because there are no doors and no windows, everything has been filled up. How could there be spaces inside?

I look and see that there are no openings in the walls. The forms are relieved only by a protruding platform that runs around, almost at the top. I feel disturbed by the notion of these vast objects being solid.

SELF Why were they filled up? Could they not be used for something.

MIDDKE AGED MAN After the war the people wanted to remove the towers, they wanted to forget what had happened, but the towers were too well built and the other houses too close. The towers could not be pulled down and they could not be dynamited, so they filled them up in order to make them useless, to make the space inside disappear. Because they have no interior the people can somehow imagine they are no longer here.

I raise the slice of bread to my mouth and inhale the fresh smell of the chives

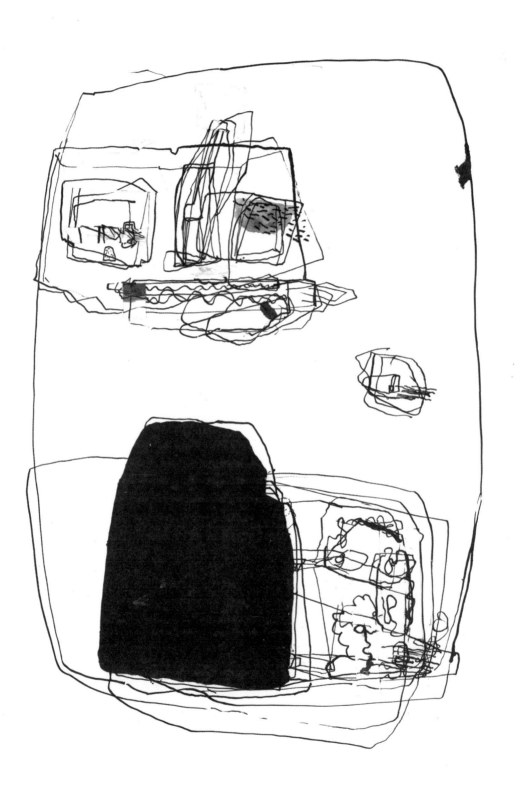

5

The Museum of Natural History

Hans-Morell-Straße 17
Siglavy

The Natural History Museum has geological, botanical,
zoological, anthropological and prehistorical collections.
The museum was arranged in the 1880s by the Darwinist
Dr Otto Hüttel. Dr Hüttel travelled to Australia,
New Zealand and the islands of the South Pacific in search
of species in the process of adaptation from one form to another.
Total number of display rooms: 27.
Total number of exhibits: 57,000.
The displays show the evolution of life from the earliest
fossil formations up to the human race. Of particular
interest are the displays of Intermediate Forms, including –
Masaoician fish with dwarf legs.
Aviterentetrix, or flying frogs.
Lesser barrier corals.
Belsamisch snails, with translucent shells.
Homo Limosus, slippery man.

I see only their coloured coats, fluorescent blues and pinks
and yellows, flashing past the doorways.

I hear the museum keepers calling out for them to be silent.

Passing through a sequence of rooms.

In the first large room, which is lined in a dark wood, are many asteroids, lying in rows in blue cupboards. In the centre stands a case with a stone as large as a man, with many silvery veins. There are diagrams, in brown ink, hard to decipher, with geometric figures showing the projected paths of the asteroids.

The second large room is painted pink and joined to the first by a pair of large doors. In this room are tubers and bulbs, mainly in glass jars. Several old women in fur coats stand in the corner, beside the heater, nibbling biscuits. They examine me suspiciously, as though I might seek to steal the biscuits.

I idle through four smaller rooms. In one a fine giraffe, with a mottled skin, indolently inspects the roses scattered along the ornamental cornices. In the second are placed wooden cases containing rows of insects, each insect mounted on a pin and neatly labelled in fading brown script, some of the insects so small as to be invisible, locatable only by their label. The high ceiling of the third room is hung with large grey-coloured birds, with long yellow beaks, their wings outstretched. The last room is filled with shoals of bright tropical fish, their scales spotted, striped, shimmering with colours that seem to reflect the artificial light.

The noise of the children's voices becomes clearer.

In a final room I stand tentatively beside a group of children. They lie on the floor with square plastic rucksacks that appear too large for them to carry. I try to move past the children, but some catch hold of my legs. I pull gently away but they hold on to my ankles, I am afraid that if I move forward or backwards I will step on them and crush them.

CHILDREN What are you doing here? Only animals are allowed in here.

They look up at me and wave their arms, while some lie on their bellies, producing large scrawled drawings in bright colours. They are drawing a case filled with skulls, the skulls decorated with roses, chequer-board patterns and florid lettering.

One boy stands beside the case and reads out the names on the skulls.

BOY Maria. Klaus. Walter. Sinni. Rudi. Lieber Norri. Wolf. Liebling. Herzchen.

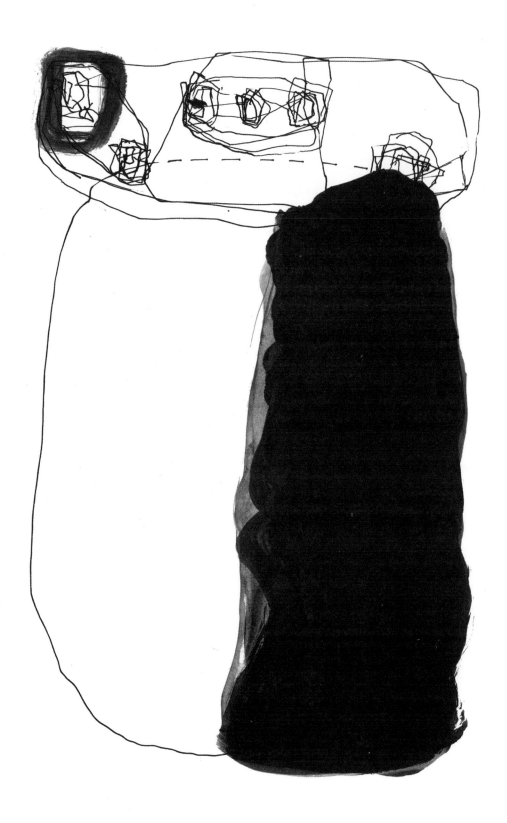

6

The Opera House

Mingenstraße 18
Neubach

*The Opera House was opened in 1876, and replaced the old opera
house on Reinsweg, which was renamed the Theatre Merinska.*
Architect: Franz von Menke.
Fixed seating: 2,300 spectators.
*Boxes: 17, including the Imperial Box with two red and gold sofas,
an iced-drinks cabinet and a metal wardrobe.*
Orchestra space: over 100 players.
*Auditorium decoration: scenes of Fulfilled Love and Frustrated
Love, by the sculptor Sacha Eugene. The notorious first
performance of Giovanni Bari's Die Sehnsucht took place here
in 1923. The unexplained death of the tenor Bernaldo Meglia,
the scandalous conduct of the mezzo-soprano Zena Pandilou,
followed by the sudden departure of Bari himself on an extensive
transatlantic tour, caused considerable controversy.*

The sound of a drawn-out nostalgic music, of violins and
accordions, a tedious trivial whining.

A large room, painted yellow, with some wooden platforms
on which are set out a number of comfortable chairs. I sink
down into the upholstery of one of the chairs, and feel almost
hidden from view.

The music shuffles on, seems to absorb refrains from familiar
tunes, half-heartedly stated then falling back, only to be
replaced by another melody. A man stands on the pavement
gesturing imploringly. It seems he is gesturing at somebody
else, who cannot be seen, who makes no response. He moves
his hands down along his face, as though drawing words out
of his mouth. A group of three, a man and two women, laugh
at the gesturing man. Another man sitting with his back to
the gesturing man, sees them laughing and turns around
to see the source of their amusement. This sitting man has a
long beard, it seems the gesturing man may be making fun
of the beard, mimicking pulling it from his face. The bearded
man becomes annoyed, he shouts. The gesturing man seems
unable to reply, he keeps on gesturing, he utters some
meaningless sounds. The bearded man appears to be unsure
of the situation, he tries to communicate, and fails. He turns
to look at me.

BEARDED MAN You.

I wonder whether I know this man. There seems to be
something familiar about him, perhaps his features, perhaps
in the line of his mouth, rather concealed behind the beard.

I scratch my head and try to look at ease.

BEARDED MAN You, please.

The music is interrupted by the sound of hammering,
followed by the whining of an electric saw.

BEARDED MAN Yes, you, if you would be so kind.

I'm sure I know this man from somewhere. I get up and walk towards him, sit down in the chair next to his.

BEARDED MAN Are you the lawyer?

SELF No, no I'm not the lawyer.

BEARDED MAN You must be the lawyer. Come on, I know you, we've met several times. What are you doing here? I thought you were still in Rotterdam.

SELF No, I've never been to Rotterdam. To Amsterdam once on holiday, to see the tulips, but never to Rotterdam.

BEARDED MAN Go back to Rotterdam. It's better to be discreet. There is nothing to see here, this isn't the right time, not yet. You must understand that if the time isn't right, then it is impossible to see anything. Later, when we contact you, everything will be clearer, we won't leave you out.

SELF But I'm not the lawyer.

The violins play a futile air.

BEARDED MAN Please, let's not discuss the matter.

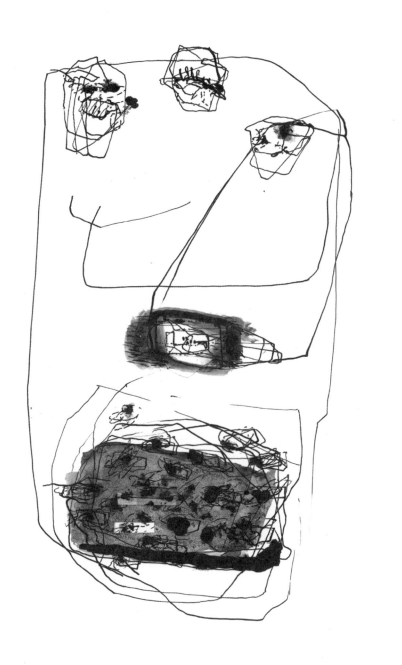

7

Museum Riedolfski

Eichengasse 18
Himmelstadt

The Museum Riedolfski, known until the war as the Haus Dilli,
is situated at the west end of the busy Eichengasse.
Construction date: 1903.
Street facade: design by Bruno Walter, sculpted figures of
nymphs, wolves, and jugglers by Fidelio Walter and Nani
Ornetto-Gültini.
Interior: rooms arranged in colour sequence based on variations
of cream, yellow and brown, the colours deepening as one
ascends the building.
Heinrich Dilli was a banker, owner of the Bank Dilli, and founder
of the Dilli Steamship Company, which undertook financial
backing for the exploration of the Central African Colonial Zone,
and the founding of the city of New W, now known as Sabara.
His eldest son Jerome was drowned in a shipping accident
on the upper reaches of the Congo. After his son's death,
Heinrich Dilli retreated from the business world and invested
his considerable fortune in paintings, concentrating on still lifes
and landscapes.

A small upstairs room.

A painting with a plain wooden frame, hanging alone. Artist not known.

A porcelain bowl, filled with raspberries lies on a narrow wooden shelf. The background is dark, part of a brown wall is visible. The berries are painted so as to appear translucent. It seems almost possible to peer through the upper layers to the fruit beneath. The small white hairs of the fruit are visible. The berries shine a bright red against the background darkness. The colour is very even, with a faint bluish sheen.

I become aware of a woman standing very close to me, looking at the painting. We are alone in the room. I hear her soft breathing. She has long dark hair and glasses with rectangular frames. She looks sideways at me for one moment. She leans towards the painting, and inhales slowly through her nose, almost as though breathing in the fragrance of the berries.

The painting seems very dark. The light is fading.
The raspberries glow as though on the point of corrupting.

The woman raises her hand slowly and points to a space before the bowl. I bend towards the picture, my mouth almost touching her hand, I see there are several tiny brightly coloured insects there, perhaps dragon flies, crawling across the board, beating their wings. The insects are painted fantastic colours, orange striped with chrome yellow, a metallic cobalt blue, they seem to be struggling against the density of the air.

POINTING WOMAN I have a theory about the little berries.

I don't exactly want to hear the theory.
I am not sure that berries require theories.

I dislike the insects, which are creeping around in an unpleasant manner.

Another woman, rather older, comes suddenly into the room, and stands by the door.

POINTING WOMAN I must go now.

SELF No, stay for a moment. I would like to know about the berries, and the theory of the berries.

Somehow the theory of the berries has now become a matter of some concern. Or rather I would like to find someone in this city with whom I can talk for a while.

POINTING WOMAN I would like to explain the theory, it is an interesting theory, but really I must go.

She smiles warmly and turns. I hear them leave, their voices becoming fainter. The room feels empty now. I look again at the picture, it seems to have grown darker, to have receded, only the creeping insects stand out. The scene has become part of a private world, separate from the one where I stand. I feel like a voyeur, peering in at some forbidden image.

8

The City Library

Erchtenweg 54
Kalksburg

*The Library was constructed by the brothers Jacob, Hensing and
Rainaldi Bellinovi, from Padua, and completed in 1724. Its form
is based on the Library of Hadrian in Athens, and consists of
a domed central space, surrounded by a number of long vaulted
rooms. A set of tunnels built within the walls allow for storage
of books and a separate circulation system for the librarians,
avoiding the necessity of passing through the reading rooms.
Number of books in the Imperial Collection: 127,000.
Colour of bindings: orange (scientific works),
brown (autobiographies), blue (romances),
yellow (stories by foreigners), pink (philosophy).
Among the celebrated volumes are -
The Ideal Atlas of Hans-Georg Henring.
The Botanical Works of Esmeamus the Younger, including
fragments of the Gioscurides Maior, with illustrations and
notes on the preparation of the varieties of edible plants.
Storia Medica Hibernica, containing a collection of treatises
on forbidden love.*

There is no space to stand in here, the ceiling curves over, the
room seems to vanish into the floor.

Three women, in dark brown dresses, sit at a metal desk, on which stand several computer monitors. With a small penknife they cut thin slices from a hard cheese, and consume them eagerly. I watch their mouths as they devour the cheese. They offer me a small piece. I place it in my mouth and chew rather nervously, it tastes salty. I imagine all our mouths close together, nibbling at the same piece of cheese, our lips barely touching, the cheese becoming smaller and smaller as our lips approach.

Through the doorway I can see into the library, a high room lined with leather bound books. A crowd of people stand and stare aimlessly, chattering amongst themselves. Beside the far wall can be seen a globe of paper, covered with large black blotches as though parts of the surface of the world had become obscured by black cloud. Against the shelves lean long step ladders mounted on wheels. The ladders curve in at the top, like gardening ladders.

The room occupied by the women is located within the thickness of the wall of the library. On one side is the weight of the books, on the other is a small window, cut at an angle into the wall, and giving a view of the sky and a roof. This roof has a zigzag pattern of grey and white, intersected once by a band of yellow. I see, at an acute angle, the pattern flickering as the shadows of passing clouds interfere with the geometry of the stripes.

One of the women, about forty years old and with blonde hair held back by a brightly-coloured plastic clip, leans forward towards me. She looks into my eyes and speaks confidentially.

WOMAN Of course our job is to look after the books, to catalogue them and put them in order. It is a very important job, because if we make a mistake, if we put here a wrong number, or perhaps erase a whole line of titles, then the books themselves would disappear, how could they be found again? Nobody reads these books now. Most are probably unreadable. You see this book, with the corners of the pages cut away. It was given to someone to read, and each time he read a page, he chopped the corner, so that he could remember how far he had got. He destroyed the book as he read it, but the effort of the reading, or the effort of the cutting, wore him down, and only about half the pages are cut away. Sometimes these books leave no space to breathe. I feel their weight on the wall, they press down into this room, that great weight on the one side and the sky on the other. Imagine if everyone who had read them had cut away a piece of each page, till there were only heaps of triangular shaped paper.

The other women pay no attention to her. They clatter with their fingers on the computer keyboards. They cut off more slices of cheese. At the side of the room is a small door opening on to a passage, the floor inclining sharply upwards. The woman leads me along a passage to a small pink room lit by a shaft of sunlight. The room is empty apart from a refrigerator and some blue plastic cups. Above the refrigerator are pinned some snapshots of landscapes, with people standing in a lake.

WOMAN I live with my husband, and my two children. My husband came out of the east zone, he left with great difficulty, we met at a dance school, and we fell in love. We never dance waltzes, that vile sluggish music is for dead people, only Spanish-American dances.

In the summer we go to the lakes. You would like it there. The lakes seem so wide but they are very shallow. You can see how funny it is, with the people standing in the centre of the lake, but the water only coming only up to their waists.

9

The Riding School

Madjesgasse 34
Jedlesee

*The Riding School was designed by Johann Stauper in the
baroque style. The central room is over 74 metres long, and
23 metres high, and is decorated with plaster friezes, with
statues of horses from Arabia, Africa, Barbary and Persia at
the four corners. The complex dressage techniques used in
performances were evolved by the cavalry officer and adventurer
Marcel Clemens, based on traditions derived from the cavalry
handbooks of the Persian empire.*
The names of the six original horses are –
Leobaldo.
Rienzi.
Fritz.
Maiolikus.
Favorin.
Meldoff.

A passage stinking of straw and sweat and shit and animals.

There are openings in the wall of the passage. I peer over the rim of one of the openings and see a large white room, with windows. The room is decorated with severe plaster mouldings. On the floor is spread neatly raked sawdust.

A rope has descended from a hole in the ceiling of the room.

From the rope, almost at ground level, hangs a vast chandelier, tier upon tier of scrolls and lights. Within the frame of the chandelier, apparently entangled in its extravagant curls, are standing a dozen men and women, balanced on chairs and step-ladders, laughing as they reach up with cloths and sponges to clean its surfaces. I walk out into the white room, and stand within the frame, as though within a small room set within the greater room, reaching upwards with my arms through the tangle of lights, immersed in the smell of the polish. One of the women offers me a small piece of cloth.

There is a slight sound from the far end of the room. All within the chandelier turn, moving awkwardly on the step-ladders, holding on to one another for support.

A large grey horse, held on a tight rein by a stout middle-aged man, stands facing us.

The horse gathers in the muscles of its body, seems to contract, then leaps directly upward without any forward motion, as though carried up by some force countering gravity. It pushes its legs outwards, the front hooves reaching out towards the chandelier, the rear hooves moving towards the face of the man holding the rein, as though to smash against his features, the man never moving, never showing any sign of even noticing. The horse somehow pauses in mid-air, held above the sawdust, then begins to contract and fold inwards, drawing its limbs back in, descending vertically to the ground.

The horse stands again on four legs, slightly puffing, swelling, its head slowly tossing. The sawdust around it lies in scattered heaps. The man still holds the rein tight.

The men and women applaud.
They coo softly.
They reach out lovingly with their bare arms towards the horse, and towards the man.
The man brushes his small black moustache with the back of his hand.

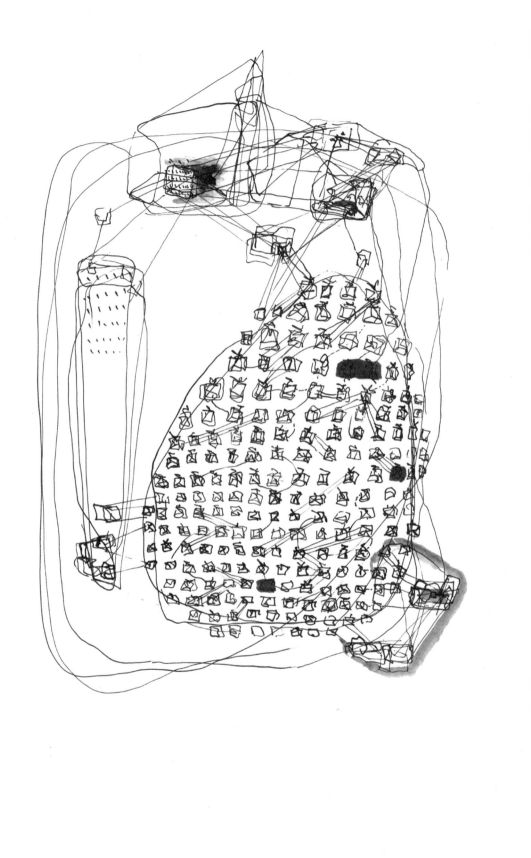

10

The Botanical Garden

Maiweg
Ost-Kopping

*The Botanical Garden, originally founded by the natural son of
the Empress Theresa, Mishka St-Doslouz, and laid out with the
assistance of the Argentinian botanist Henry Bellamy, contains
specimens of plants from all over the world. The layout of the
garden is based on the seven great rivers of the world, each river
being represented by a serpentine canal, all the canals joining
in a circular ornamental lake.*
*The display of plants from the lands of the former empire,
includes –*
Moga trees.
Albus Albus (unique specimen).
Sahara berries.
Craeanthiae.
Over 14,000 alpine plants.
*The Central Conservatory, erected in 1874, is 108 metres long,
and heated by a unusual gas-circulation system.*

A device for watering plants, functioning in irregular spurts.

On the terrace of a small brick building is laid out a display of several hundred apparently identical rock-plants, each in a small terracotta pot. I see some gardeners.

SELF How can all these plants be told apart?

The gardeners consider the situation.

FIRST GARDENER Yes, the plants all seem the same at first. There seems to be no difference between one plant and another, let alone the possibility of naming that difference. Even, possibly, there may be no difference, just a need to call them different. These plants come from another land where the air is drier and colder, where there are only rocks as far as you can see. Sometimes, if you get down on your knees and try to see down into the cracks, into the long narrow crevices which run through this whole landscape, there are the flowers, very bright pinks and yellows hidden away in the gloom. An empty landscape, where everything is so isolated where nothing seems really to belong. In such a landscape there is nothing on which the mind can fix, only a kind of drifting. When the plants come down here, when they sit in the pots, they begin to change, they no longer have the same emptiness, they are not the plants they were before. The labels begin to lose their meaning as plants that seem similar diverge, we have to think of new names.

She points to the leaves of one small plant, her voice tails off at the thought of this task. I ask her where this landscape is located.

FIRST GARDENER In the mountains to the west.

The second gardener, who has been looking increasingly frustrated breaks in.

SECOND GARDENER Rocks, rocks, rocks. All you speak about is rocks and emptiness. Radishes, I grow radishes. See their wonderful bulging forms. Such reds and purples, sometimes even almost blue. Can you believe such colours exist under the earth, waiting to be found.

The three of us stroll along the terrace, myself in the centre, a gardener on either side.

SECOND GARDENER Everyday I work here. I become tired of plants, even of radishes. I watch the women coming by. I am kneeling down and I look up at them. Or, better, I am up a tree and looking down at them. Or, best, I stand by the path, holding my hoe. No-one really sees a gardener, people just seem to think of us as another plant here, with no existence beyond the garden. Sometimes they ask me a question, what is this plant, or is this the way to the exit, and I pause for a long time, because then they begin to look at me a little, and people expect gardeners to be a little slow, and I look into their eyes and nod a little.

The first gardener is shaking her head, the second gardener appears deeply involved in his subject. I begin to feel the matter of the identical plants is becoming no clearer. I wonder whether the gardeners themselves are no more knowledgeable about the question than myself, and feel my own interest in the subject waning. I notice a third gardener lying on her back in a wheelbarrow, arms and legs hanging casually over the rim. This figure appears to have little to say. The sun shines on her face, and on her contentedly closed eyes.

There is a pause in the conversation. With the first two gardeners I stand beside the wheelbarrow. The three of us look down on the sleeping form. The first gardener tenderly runs her middle finger down the bridge of the nose of the sleeping woman.

11

House Chaink

Am Spittelhügel 14
Webbing

*The triangular Haus Chaink was erected in 1934 by the paper
manufacturer Gottfried Chaink who had made a considerable
fortune based on his monopoly of paper supplies to the government
services. The house features several rooms designed by his daughter,
the mathematician Isabel Chaink. It is believed that the proportions
of these rooms are an exposition of certain numerical series, known
to mathematicians as Chaink Series, expanded into volumetric form.
Primitive Chaink series: 3 8 14 21 22 4 5 9 11 17 2 etc.
The notes of Frau Chaink have been lost. Hints as to the
nature of these numerical series, with their curious regressive
developments, have been preserved in the records of
conversations with Frau Chaink in the diaries of the musician
Christof Belling, whose own compositions were based on similar
mathematical structures. Most of the Chaink family fled W
shortly after the imposition of the Racial Purity Laws in 1938.
The house was seized. Her two uncles and an aunt remained
behind in W, and were taken to the camps. Isabel Chaink
settled in Vancouver, but died after a year of exile.
Uses of Chaink House by fascist authorities –
Army barracks.
Bottle store.
Detention centre.
The house is at present used by the Mexican Consulate.*

She tried to make all the pieces of the wooden floor fit together.

She measured, calculating the proportions, attempting to hold everything together in a single system, controlled by the numbers of the series.

On the wall hangs a photograph of three young men standing in the woods, laughing. The men wear hunting clothes and boots. A little to one side stand two women, also in hunting jackets and trousers. One of the men carries a rifle.

A middle-aged woman paces the room nervously. She smokes, inhaling and exhaling through her teeth, and speaks to me in short sentences inserted into this rhythm of breathing.

WALKING WOMAN I knew her well, she was happy in love. But after the Purity Laws, the man grew more distant. He was a weak man and afraid, all the men of this city are weak and afraid.

The floor is constructed of small panels of oak and maple. The wood panels bear signs of heavy objects having been moved across them, and are sometimes deeply rutted.

WALKING WOMAN She could never work out the pattern of the floor so that it fitted the room. There was something about the number series that didn't fit the room. Perhaps it was the fact that the numbers moved not only forwards but also backwards. Her family thought her unhappy in love, they asked why it was so important that the room fitted the series. They just wanted a room to live in, some sunshine, somewhere to put the sofa. But she thought that the numbers meant something, that they could exist in the ordinary world, and that when they became a space which could be inhabited, when their qualities were clearly revealed, then everybody would understand. She was trying to create a volume out of an idea. Over here in the corner, if you look carefully, you

can see how distorted the shapes are. It upset her at first
that the series didn't hold things together, that it needed to
be distorted. She became very disturbed. She sat upstairs in
the small room, drawing on pieces of tracing paper, making
figures out of thread and pins. The workers building the room
refused to co-operate any more, they had built it so often, and
then had to dismantle the pieces because it was never quite
correct. They didn't understand what she was saying, because
they came from the eastern provinces, where the people speak
a different dialect. Or they pretended not to understand.
They claimed their tools were not accurate enough for cutting
the timber into such precise shapes, they became tired of
her sulking and her violent temper, and prepared to leave.
They had to be bribed with money and food to come back,
and even then they could never really put the pieces together
properly. But in the end she realised it didn't matter, what
held the room together wasn't merely the numbers or the
dimensions, but a kind of balance between the pieces, between
their surfaces.

I feel unable to understand the complicated system behind
the room. Judging various points of the floor against the size
of my shoe, I see that what the woman says is true, that the
pattern which had seemed orthogonal is in fact distorted.

SELF With whom was she in love?

WALKING WOMAN A businessman, the manager of a factory for
the manufacture of matchsticks. You can see him there in the
photograph, holding the rifle.

SELF What became of the maker of matchsticks?

WALKING WOMAN It is really of no importance what became
of the maker of matchsticks.

12

The Narrenhaus

Altes Krankenhaus
Brummering

*The Narrenhaus, House of Fools, was constructed in 1773 for
the confinement of the insane, on the orders and following the
designs of the Emperor Rudolf. It lies in the grounds of the
Old Hospital, which has subsequently been converted into a hotel.
Form: circular.
Height of tower: 24 metres.
Number of floors: 6.
Number of cells per floor: 28.
Equipment in each cell: a bed, a chain, a small metal bowl.
In the central courtyard is constructed a building for the
warders. The Narrenhaus is surrounded by a small garden,
laid out with cedars and pines.*

Walking around the curve of each corridor.

On one side the little windows looking into the central shaft, on the other the heavy timber doors, with small barred windows. The view along the corridor is cut off by the curve of the wall, confined but always the same, the little windows, the timber doors. Going up a floor, going down, the corridors only repeat. Only the light begins to change, from the sunless gloom of the lower levels, to the thin rays of light slipping through the southern windows of the upper levels.

All divided, all arranged.
On the east side the female patients.
On the west the male.
On the lower floors the curable, at the highest levels the incurable and the violent.
Ascending higher into delusion.

The rotation of the sun around the tower.
A shaft of sunlight stretching into the room.
Marking the length of the shaft of light.
The shaft forming a space pushed in from outside.
The shaft never still, but moving with the days and seasons.
Shady days. No shaft.
Days missing.
Days crossed off on the wall, using a piece of metal.

The Emperor visits the Narrenhaus on sunny days and ascends to the roof, from which he can look out over the surrounding town, kept safe from the insane. The tops of the cedars are almost the same height as the top of the tower. He walks around the circular path on the roof, dressed in his heavy uniform, and his black triangular hat with the yellow plumes, accompanied by a few choice companions, and perhaps by the doctors who expound on the more interesting cases. He follows the individual cases, and listens carefully to accounts of the progress of the inmates.

DOCTORS They cannot be cured.

EMPEROR These also are my subjects. I am their father.

MAD MAN Father, no father.

He sometimes hears terrible cries and weeping from below.
Occasionally he speaks to the calmer cases, gives encouragement.

Hearing his voice but not listening.

To escape from the circle of the corridor into the quiet of the
cell. Not to move. The ceiling of massive masonry, curved over,
enclosing, holding. To lie on the wooden bed, head pointing
to the centre, toes outward, facing west. Thoughts tumbling
round in head. All the jumbled, disordered thoughts that
occurred here before, by others, lying so. Tired of counting.
Figures never adding up. Looking out through the window,
no town, no people, no woods, a thin blue sky, a streak of white
cloud across the space of the window, gradually spreading out
into thin strands, curling, dispersing.

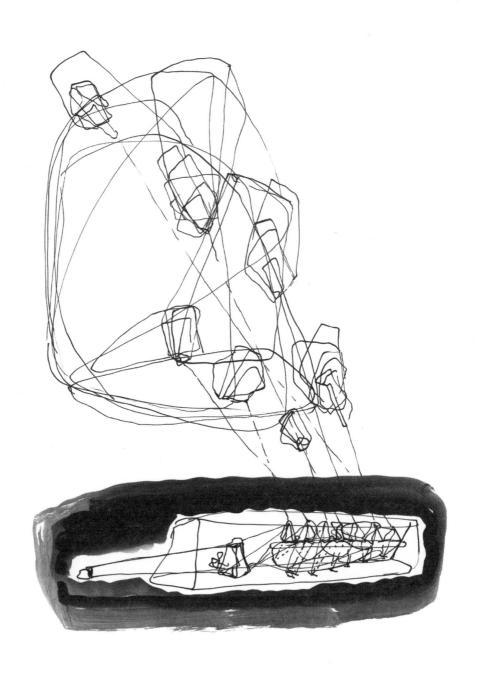

13

Monument to the Heroes of the Uprising

Josef-Schweibler-Straße
Speising

The monument was created by the sculptor Frantisec Merula, to
commemorate the massacre following the uprising in September
1907 by workers of the Luisedorf district, in protest against the
wage cuts imposed by the military government. Funds for the
monument were raised by public subscription, a special casting
chamber was erected by members of the metal workers' union
for the casting of the unusually large elements. During the period
of fascist rule efforts were made to destroy the statue. For some
years it was concealed by a wooden scaffolding.
Material: bronze.
Weight: 137 tonnes.
Height: 14 metres.
Length: 23 metres.
Date of erection: 1928.
Loss of life in the uprising of 1907: 73 men, 12 women.

One carries a banner, others cry out.

Standing on a great stone plinth, the giant figures stride forward, their arms outstretched. Some appear to be collapsing backwards from their wounds, others blown about by a wind that pulls their clothes into drawn-out forms.

A group of men and women, dressed in heavy coats and denim jackets, sit on a bench, talking and drinking from bottles of beer. They are surrounded by rows of empty beer bottles and cardboard cartons. One man gets up and walks aside, urinates.

Behind the monument, and stretching out on either side, are planted laurel bushes. I walk around the back of the monument. In the plinth is a small metal door, propped open. Within lies a large room. In the doorway stands an old man, wearing only a pair of rough grey trousers, held up by a leather belt. He is shaving himself with a blue plastic razor, moving the razor carefully over the folds of his face. The old man turns towards me, one eye lazily following the other, and gestures impatiently with the razor.

OLD MAN Go away. Can't you see I'm busy.

The interior of the plinth is filled with tools for gardening, and metal drums. Amongst them stand two stone statues of squat athletes, each carrying a discus. On a metal bench sit a woman and two younger men. The woman combs her long red hair.

SELF Do you live here?

OLD MAN Of course I don't live here. Why should I live in a monument? No-one lives in a monument. I have a fine house.

SELF And what kind of house would that be?

OLD MAN A very fine house. A person like you cannot imagine such a house. Made of stone. Built by my father. And I myself have built parts. With several fine rooms. With plaster ceilings. One with a frieze of angel heads, so that you feel already in paradise. Also with a colour television set, a washing machine, and a garage. And a terrace for sitting out on summer evenings and watching the sun go down. The house lies in a valley, amongst the pine trees. Below the house is a field for the animals. Such fine cows, fine pigs, and fine horses.

WOMAN WITH RED HAIR And you? Do you have such a fine house?

SELF No, I have only a flat.

WOMAN WITH RED HAIR And do you have a field with cows and pigs and horses?

SELF No. I don't have much space for animals.

I notice at the rear of the room a ladder leading up into some space above the plinth.

SELF Is it possible to go up into the monument?

WOMAN WITH RED HAIR Entry to the monument is restricted to visitors with authorisation from the correct authorities.

SELF Who are the correct authorities?

WOMAN WITH RED HAIR That is not our concern.

14

The Woods

A Path in the Woods
Malzing

*The woods within the city boundaries of W extend into the
surrounding hills and countryside. The trees are mostly oaks,
chestnuts, beeches and limes. Routes through these woods are
marked out with coloured bands painted on the trees.*
Red bands: route to Ubbswasser.
Blue bands: route to Schloß Ivanov and Salernico.
Orange bands: route to Cincinatini Nature Reserve.
Green bands: route to vineyards.
White bands: route to lakes.
*Within the woods are constructed wooden observation towers for
hunters. These towers are slightly lower than the surrounding
tree line. Typical wildlife to be seen in the woods include –*
Elpichian Deer.
Dibo Rats.
Red Hares.
Rheinhards Beast.
Alpine Jackdaws and Cis-alpine Jackdaws.

Follow the orange bands.

On a rise are set out some wooden tables and chairs. Men with electric meat cutters slice up animals. Behind the trees large motor cars are visible.

A group of men and women sit at the table. The men wear light summer suits, shirts and ties. The women have dresses of expensive material, elegant hats and fine leather bags. On the table are glasses and bottles of white wine. One of the men comes forward and embraces me, my friend, yes, my friend. He takes me to my place at the table. I sit down, I appear to be amongst friends. You are American? asks a women with very short hair. Ah from England, I was in England too, by the sea, the English humour, it is so famous, many amusing things, always laughing, but from the outside, from far away. Here we live here on the inside, at the centre.

A man with long brown hair, tied back with a ribbon, stands up. He speaks loudly and rather formally.

MAN WITH BROWN HAIR Today is the anniversary of the founding of the city. A Roman general, sometimes said by some to be a woman, an unlikely eventuality, but certainly very noble, even if also occasionally said to be of North African origin, maybe even dark-skinned, is lost in the woods. He is accompanied only by a few soldiers. He sees in the distance a large animal, luminous white in colour, running through the woods. The soldiers set off through the forest, following the white form, pushing their way through the thickness of the forest. At last the animal halts on a small rise beside the river, and the soldiers surround it. They cut down branches and build a rough stockade around the animal. They fall asleep, listening to the sound of the animal's feet on the undergrowth.

The man pauses.
The cooks throw the meat on to a barbecue rack.

The woman whispers into my ear.
I feel the warmth of her breath on my skin.

WHISPERING WOMAN Only the men would tell such stories.
Soldiers and stags and generals. We were waiting for you,
we wanted you to come and be with us, we thought you had
mistaken the path in the woods.

MAN WITH BROWN HAIR In the morning, the stockade is empty,
the animal is gone. The soldiers construct a small platform
of stones. The general stands on the platform and speaks.
The animal, he says, is a sign. A city will be constructed here,
in honour of the Emperor.

The others grouped at the table sing a short, cheerful tune.
I wish to sing with them, but do not know the words. I turn
to the woman beside me.

SELF But it is not clear what happened to the animal.

WOMAN The animal is not important, only the English would
worry about the animal.

SELF I wish it were clearer.

WOMAN It is perfectly clear. The animal disappears. The city
is founded. The one replaces the other. You shouldn't look for
too many explanations.

The brown-haired man overhears.
The cooks add aromatic herbs to the meat.
Magpies rustle in the branches.

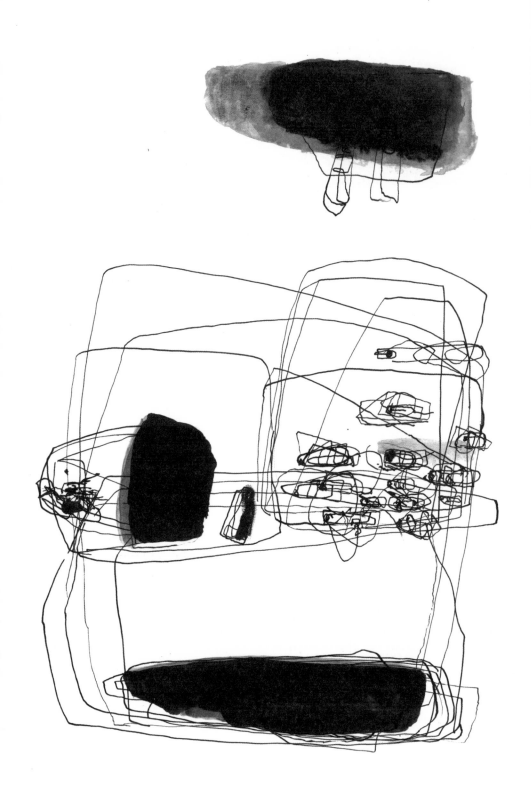

15

Höbbelsalon

Kunzepark
Theresastadt

The salon was founded in 1880 by the dance master Alfred
Höbbel. The series of lavish rooms, decorated with images of
mythological scenes, are extended in the summer period with
outdoor wooden platforms. The salon is dedicated to the dancing
of the waltz, and a small orchestra plays waltz music here in the
evenings. It is situated at the southern end of the Kunzepark,
the paths leading to the building are marked by statues of the
celebrated musicians of W, including –
Alfred Maisnitz: beside the path to the canal.
Christof Belling: in the grove of cherry trees.
Miguel Cirena: beside the octagonal pond.
Sarah Wollf: entrance to the rose garden.
Frederik Karas: entrance to the rose garden.

A girl with thin legs sings a melancholic Russian song. She
has long scratches on her legs.

WAITER WITH SHINY POINTED SHOES You can't come in and not pay. You must order something. Some water. You want only water? We don't serve water.

A dark room. Searching for the light switch. The light sizzles when it is switched on, as though water is running over the socket. Is there someone else in the room? A man and a woman coming in. Very late. The sound of hurried breathing. Don't open the door, don't open the door.

The waiter becomes confused, he can't remember to which table he should bring the beer, but he doesn't care. With his metal-framed glasses he looks a little like my younger brother. The police arrive and begin to push through the crowd.

POLICE Who has seen Herr Dieter? Don't be anxious, all will be well.

OTHERS I haven't seen Herr Dieter. Who is Herr Dieter? I don't even know Herr Dieter.

POLICE You must know Herr Dieter. We have been told you know Herr Dieter.

SELF It's a mistake, you must be looking for someone else.

POLICE Over here, bring the light over here. We must find Herr Dieter.

OTHERS Be quiet.

LEADER OF THE ORCHESTRA And now we will play an old tune by a well-loved composer from this city, The Girls of the River, by Christof Belling.

Asian girls dressed in alpine costumes waltz with men in dark
suits. The girls have fixed smiles, they seem to dance in a
trance. Suddenly one laughs, her head on one side, her teeth
flashing white.

No no, I can't dance like that.
I don't know how to move my feet.
Yes, it's easy for you, but not for me.

POLICE Herr Dieter, please Herr Dieter.

The horns blow sentimentally.
A man in a shirt with bright dayglo flowers slips.
He is held up by the couples around him.
He opens his mouth wide.
They call his name and kiss his face.
They stroke his chest.

OTHERS Hold him, hold him.

OTHERS Don't let him go.

Hold me here.
Arms, legs.
Feet moving across the floor.
Faster, faster.
Moving around and around.

16

Museum des Unglaubens

Schlesingerstraße 9
Conversano

The Museum des Unglaubens is located in the former Palais
Pichilitsch, a two storey building with an exterior of green stucco.
The Museum contains documents and relics from the period of
the Oriental Wars, including –
Armour with enamel inlay.
Devices for the calculation of mortar trajectories.
Soldiers' letters.
Folding armchairs and tables for use in the field.
Miniature paintings with scenes of soldiers with female camp
followers.
Banners.
At one point in the wars, W was besieged by the Oriental Army,
which seemed on the point of seizing the city, but suddenly, and
for no clear reason, withdrew.

A large room, smelling of floor polish. The walls painted
a hygienic green, the lights fluorescent and functional.

On the wall hangs a row of large glazed plates, showing men in long patterned robes.

A bored attendant reads a copy of the daily newspaper. Moustache, neatly trimmed. Small blue eyes, glancing sideways.

Within the image on one of the plates sits the Sultan Suleyman, seen in profile. Suleyman wears a large turban, folded in a complex fashion around his head. He peers out through narrow eye slits. He is seated in a wicker chair, placed upon a carpet.

The attendant sniffs loudly and blows his nose into a yellow handkerchief.

Behind the sultan, on the border of the carpet, stands the Armenian interpreter, taller than the sultan but drooping slightly, perhaps to indicate his inferior position. Further in the background lies a hill with a walled city. Some troops, carrying coloured umbrellas, are riding away from the city.

The attendant comes and stands beside me. Without being asked, he begins to tell me of the dream of the sultan on the last night of the siege.

ATTENDANT I am hungry. I sit beside the wall of the city, in the shade. I see two pots, a red pot and a green pot, but even though I reach out for them I cannot touch them. A man with a red face sits beside the red pot and a man with a green face beside the green pot. They each offer me food from their pot, but warn that the food from the other pot is poisoned. I reach out first to the one, then to the other. I cannot choose. I see the whiteness of my hands. I realise I do not know the colour of my own face. By closing my right eye I can see my nose through my left eye, it seems red. But by closing my left eye I can see through my right eye that my nose seems tinged with green. I smell the odour of the spices. I feel the hunger in my stomach. The men are using large knives to hack at small cloves of nutmeg.

The attendant wipes his nose again. I look at the image of the sultan. He seems tired, and to be waiting for something to occur. He is looking down at the palm of his left hand, rubbing the thumb of his right hand on the flesh. The interpreter shades the sultan's head with an umbrella. The sultan seems to turn his head a little, upwards and sideways, to see the interpreter.

I half close my eyes to check on my own nose. I notice that it can only be seen with any clarity by closing one eye and staring at one side of the nose, and then repeating the process for the other side. The two views appear not to be symmetrical, though I am uncertain whether this is due to some peculiarity of my nose, or of my eyes. The flesh, at least, appears to be of a normal colour.

The attendant looks at me with a certain air of knowing something. He returns to his chair, and stares at me as though awaiting some comment on his story. I search the pictures on the plates for a sign of the two men with the pots. They are not there. I hear the sound of the folding of newspaper. The attendant looks at me again and stretches his arms. He examines his watch. I begin to rather dislike his air of self-confidence. I decide to ignore him. I wonder if there is coffee available in the museum. He takes from his jacket pocket an object wrapped in greaseproof paper, unwrapping it to reveal a hard-boiled egg. He taps the shell of the egg gently against his knee.

17

Haus Reiner

Meinikeweg 14
Krebling

*The Haus Reiner was once the residence of the physician
Dr Jean-Nikolas Reiner. On the first floor were conducted
experiments in corporal magnetism, in an effort to restore
the eyesight of blind people. Dr Reiner gained great fame
and a small fortune from these experiments. However the
experiments were criticised by other doctors on the grounds
that the patients were unable to give the correct names to
the objects they saw, and that many of the patients were of
low class origin and thus unreliable.*
Objects used in Dr Reiner's optical identification tests –
Blue glass sphere.
White glass rod.
Wooden cube.
Wooden sphere.
Metal fork.
Metal hoop.
*It was also rumoured that Dr Reiner was emotionally
involved with certain of his female patients. He was forced
to leave W for Paris. In the museum on the first floor there
is a small display of ophthalmic and other instruments.*
The house is now divided up into small flats.

We sit with our knees almost touching. She seems very
uncertain, and speaks, in English, very quietly. I realise
that I make her nervous.

A conversation with an aunt. The flat in the attic of the Haus Reiner. On the table beside us, two white ceramic plates.

SELF Why did we always call you 'aunt'? You are not really an aunt, are you?

AUNT No, how could I be your aunt. It was just a way of speaking. Perhaps your father wanted me to be part of the family.

SELF It must have meant something.

AUNT He liked me. Perhaps he thought I would never have any children of my own. Everybody was getting married then, after the war, having children. What a pity my children aren't here now, they would have certainly liked to have met you.

SELF Maybe you were a kind of second mother.

AUNT Not for you. You are somebody else's child. Why should I be given somebody else's child?

SELF No, certainly there is no reason to be given someone else's child.

AUNT And do you think you need two mothers?

SELF One is really adequate.

AUNT Look at the photograph of my own children, over there.

SELF Yes, I see them. I wanted only to find out what my family were doing in W.

AUNT I never wanted to be an aunt. Why should anyone wish to be an aunt?

SELF I can think of no clear reason.

AUNT Why does it matter what your family were doing in W. Nobody would remember them now. It was a long time ago, and they are not here any more. Probably it was to do with the Russians.

SELF What was it do with Russians?

AUNT The Russians, your family, everybody disappearing.

SELF I don't understand. Who disappeared?

AUNT People. Many of the people we knew. They were there and then they were not there, and soon nobody could even say that they had ever been there. When so many have disappeared it becomes impossible to speak, it is dangerous to speak, and anyway there is really nobody left to speak to. Even when other people come, even when people stop disappearing, it is still not possible to speak. The habit of not speaking has grown too strong. It doesn't matter now. Come out on to the terrace. We can sit here, in the sun. You see, it's like a garden, a garden in England. We have geraniums in pots. They need more sunshine really, but the sun only comes here in the evening, when it comes past that big sign. Can you see the sign?

SELF It appears to be a picture of cowboys.

AUNT Yes, cowboys, or at least men on horses. We must certainly talk about everything. You must tell me all the amusing things that have happened to you.

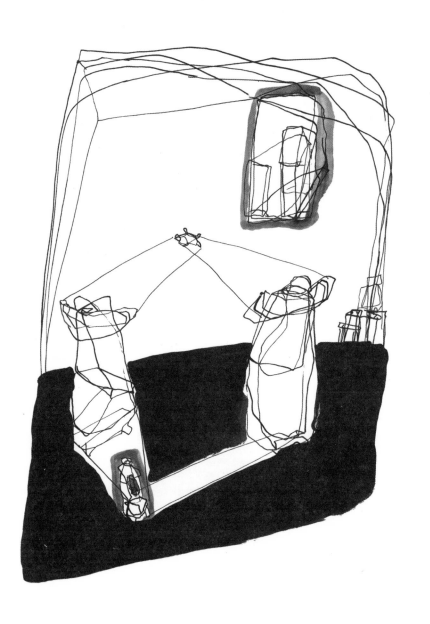

18

Konditorei Mailand

Kwapilweg 39
Rosenau

*The residential district of Rosenau is laid out with attractive
tree-lined streets. Its notable inhabitants have included the
musician Frederik Karas, Sonia Mailski, the discoverer of the
inert gas Gargon, and the linguist Michael Sinder, who studied
the emergence of the W dialect from its sources amongst the
various nationalities of the inhabitants, attempting to find the
speech of the original inhabitants. The Kwapilweg is noted for
the high quality of its cake shops and coffee houses, where the
writers and idlers of the city still meet. Konditorei Mailand is
celebrated for its sugared delicacies, including –
Torte Vreblinka.
Rosahimmelkuchen.
Pichilitschkuchen.
Kaiser-Rudolf-Mandeln.
Hasetraumkuchen, with pale yellow icing and a filling of marzipan
flavoured with Amarillo, that is prepared only at Easter time.*

The baby flies through the air, and as it flies it screams, with
a mixture of pleasure and fear.

I sit at the small metal table by the door, and consume a cake filled with blueberries.

BABY Eeeeeh.

Katya Pubelski, cook.
Irene her sister.
Both refugees from Galicia. They teach the children songs, mostly happy repetitive ditties, sometimes accompanied by gestures.

In the kitchen stands a wooden table. On the table sits a wooden board, on which lie flattened rolls of chocolate, dried fruit peel and nuts. There is a heavy drowsy smell of the warm chocolate and of cinnamon. The nuts are sliced with a curved knife, rolled back and forth across the board. A fruit tart cools on a shelf beside the open window.

The two women stand, one on either side of the room, and they throw the baby between them. It flies up, it lands in their arms and is safe, and then it is in the air again and I think it will fall and be killed, that it will slip. Maybe I even hope that it will slip and crash on the floor, and stop this screaming. But it lands safe and they all laugh and the baby howls for more, and all laugh, so more.

Through the half-open door, it is possible to see a vertical slot of space with the window and the windows behind, then just the form of the baby appearing for one moment in this slot and vanishing.

Katya comes out, wiping her hands on her apron. She picks up another child, about eight years old and dressed in pink floral shirt and shorts.

BOY And me, you have forgotten me!

KATYA No, I love you, I love you so much, you are always my little favourite. How could I ever forget my favourite?

BOY Show me you love me best.

She stands him on a chair and feeds him small pieces of chocolate and nuts. He closes his eyes and opens his mouth for more, making small bird-like noises.

Hoping the baby has been forgotten.

19

Bahnhof Franz-Joseph

Franz-Joseph-Platz
Mariagrund

The Franz-Joseph railway station has seventeen platforms.
The famous rail-viaduct, constructed using a spanning technique
derived from Byzantine churches, was built by the Scots engineer
Alexander McFarlane, of the Lowlands and Plains Rail
Company. On the facade of the station are terracotta reliefs
depicting scenes in the various cities of the empire –
PRAG: citizens on horseback.
BUDAPEST: women bathing.
VENEDIG: houses being transported on barges.
TRIEST: doctors examining patient.
KRAKAU: the enthronement of the archbishop.
NEU W: natives welcoming explorers arriving in a steamship.
The station was opened in 1894 with a ceremonial dinner, lit by
gas flares, to which 3,000 dignitaries were invited. The orchestra,
led by the virtuoso violinist Arabelle Vreblink, arrived on
a flatbed truck pulled by a Sallivich steam locomotive, and
performed the Dance of the Dwarves from Miguel Cirena's
New W Symphony.

The illuminated signboard shows destinations not recorded
on the city map.

Somewhere underground. A long empty space, lit by dim lamps. Figures moving restlessly. Empty trains passing by slowly.

Two ragged women stand beside me, laden down with plastic bags. They push prams with large babies in them, the babies waving their arms and gesturing.

The women remain silent, glum.

The babies throw diverse coloured articles out of the pram, they shriek and gurgle. The women try to recover the articles, which roll around on the platform.

MOTHERS Babies, be still.

A train halts. Some old ladies, wearing hats and carrying large leather bags, dismount. They try to push past between me and the ragged women.

OLD LADIES Away, away.

The ragged women hold out their hands for money, and speak in an irregular monotone, as though narrating an oft-told story.

MOTHERS We need money, for our babies.

OLD LADIES Out of our way.

MOTHERS We have lost everything in the war... babies... babies.

OLD LADIES Babies? You call these monsters babies? Look how they are too big for their prams. Let us through, if you don't let us through we will call the police.

The old ladies push through, and walk smartly away. The ragged women become more aggressive and shout after them.

I consider myself somehow included in the old ladies' disgust, and feel also a certain satisfaction with this inclusion. I look down at the babies and move to a more central position. I am almost part of the family. I also have been insulted by this high-handed treatment. This relationship is however in no way acknowledged by the ragged women, who begin to comb their hair, paying me no attention.

We wait together. A kind of lethargy seems to have settled over us. It becomes an effort to move, or even to think of leaving. Even if the correct train were to arrive, nobody would board it to leave.

More trains pass by.

I consider that these are very fine babies, though it is difficult to know what sex or nationality they are.

The babies, moving together with a ponderous sense of purpose, point upwards at the roof of the station, and stare, spittle dribbling from their mouths.

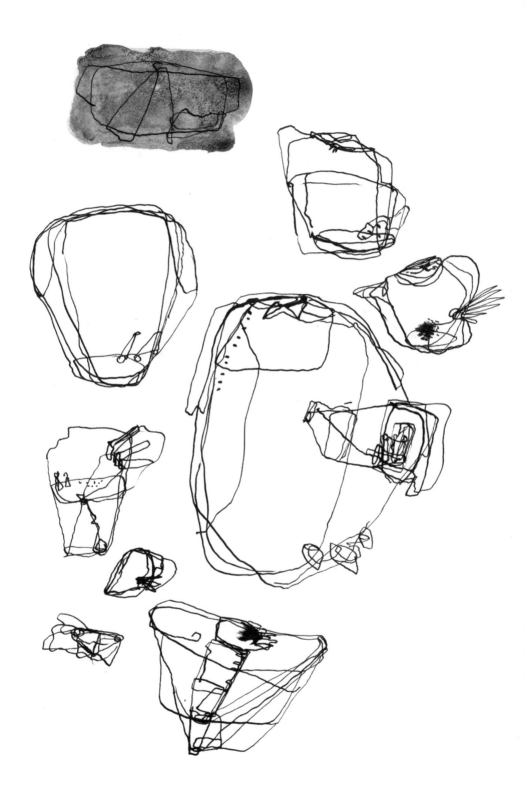

20

Men's Outfitters

Klischniggasse 17
Möhning-Steindorf

The area of Möhning-Steindorf is dominated by the twin towers
of the offices of the Organisation of International Friendship.
The building was the scene of a terrorist outrage in 1982 in which
several bystanders were killed and the President of the Republic,
Rolf Kluckman, was badly wounded. The nearby Klischniggasse
is a centre for the clothing industry and men's outfitters.
The actress Liese Düppel, star of many post-war movie dramas,
was born at Klischniggasse 24. She later moved to Hollywood,
and married in turn –
The director Oscar Minnotie.
The real estate investor Raymond Zinko.
The co-star of her movie St Maxim Day, Ernest Mayway.
The Republican politician and Governor of Nevada, Richard
Valmez.

A shop window with several suits, hats, pairs of trousers.
Within the shop two assistants bow slightly and see to the
customers' demands. To the side, a man operates a sewing
machine amidst piles of clothing.

On a rack at the back of the shop is hung a line of second-hand clothing, left for repairs and not reclaimed. I sort through the rack and select a pair of grey flannel trousers with the label Cambridge Men's Clothing, Articles of Quality. In one of the pockets of the trousers is a hand-written note.

The note is written in German, in pencil, on graph paper apparently torn from a notebook. It reads:

I can imagine a sighted man in a tribe of blind people, and this man trying to describe the sensation of seeing to those around him. How will this man describe what he sees, what terms will he use?

I try on the trousers. They are made of fine material but are rather too short in the leg.

I show the note to one of the assistants. He puts on his glasses, and reads it carefully. He considers the question, and shows the note to the other assistant.

FIRST ASSISTANT Who is it then that imagines this man? Who is writing this note, and leaving it here in the pockets of trousers to be found and to confuse us? Some philosopher, as if this city were not already filled with enough philosophers. If this philosopher writes he must be a sighted man, because blind men, so far as I know cannot write. And if he is sighted then who does he consider blind, is it all of us, is he the only one that can see, and all of us only think we see, we are under some delusion of sight, but really we don't see, and we have no knowledge of this situation, because we are all the same, it doesn't matter what we lack if we all lack, it doesn't matter because we don't even know there is something the matter, and then along comes this man, who thinks that he can see, and he alone in this tribe, and leaves notes in the trousers of other people, notes that are found by others, notes that we can read, because we are after all not as blind as that. Notes that imply, because this is only suggestion, a sly encroaching suggestion, that there is something else worth seeing, another way of seeing, which, of course, we will never obtain, because we can never see, but which we can only read about, which we can only experience second-hand, from someone else who really can see, or says, or implies, that he really can see, and then suggests, yes this note is all suggestion, that there might be no way that he could tell us what this seeing really is, because there are no words to describe it. How could he describe something that is beyond what we can see? How can he say it is blue, when we have no idea what blue is? This whole question is a taunting, a threat, a subversion, sent, or rather left, here in these trousers, which are after all a fine cut and of very fine stuff, and not at all expensive, a very fair price when all is said. Left here to unsettle us, to worry us. And this man, or woman for it is just as likely that a woman would do something like this, even if this is a man's shop, perhaps even more likely a woman who intends to unsettle us men, well whoever it is that leaves such a note, no, we will not be worried by such a thing, by such a taunting.

He pauses for breath.

SECOND ASSISTANT But... But... But...

He moves his arms slowly in circles, describing great arcs of space, as he struggles to speak.

The first assistant screws up the note, opens the shop door and throws it outside.

The second assistant holds out his hand, one finger uplifted, he turns towards me, a great smile begins to spread across his face.

21

Bathing Resort

Gauler-Insel
Limming

The construction of a new staightened course for the river Dibo
in 1838, with the aim of easing navigation, left isolated the old
bend of the river, a stretch of water over two kilometres long.
On the banks and on the islands were erected various bathing
places, which became very fashionable in the last quarter of the
nineteenth-century. The celebrated modernist diving boards,
in ferrous cement, are by the Italian engineer Rainaldo Sverro.
Amongst the bathing cabins are those designed in the 1930s by
the architect Ernst Dangobel. They are constructed of wood and
aluminium and decorated in bright yellows, blues and whites.
In the final years of the war the cabins were used as temporary
housing for those whose homes had been destroyed. The occupants
of the cabins used the surrounding land for the growing of
vegetables, and the grazing of sheep.

The small grey fish. Fear of the long tresses of the grey brown
weeds, which conceal the river-bed.

Swimming under the water, looking up. The sunlight penetrating the muddy water, illuminating flecks of algae. The uncertain forms of the other swimmers, suddenly seen, their bare legs kicking underwater.

On the water floats a wooden launch, its name written on the stern in Cyrillic script. Two men sit in the boat.

Beside the water's edge are a row of small timber cabins, painted a bleached pale blue. I sit on a wooden bench and dry myself in the sun. On a flat wooden bed lies an old man, naked, wearing sun-glasses with bright yellow frames. Beside him, in the shade, sits an old woman, playing patience.

PATIENCE-PLAYING WOMAN The kings are all missing.

They pay little attention to one another. The man lights a cigarette and carefully makes a small mark on the cigarette packet.

The sound of rock music on the radio, a metallic dance melody, with a wailing female singer.

Two children stand before the man, both wearing red bathing trunks. The smaller boy dances to the music, jerking his head and singing the words. They talk to the man, moving their arms as though encouraging him to do something. At first he is silent, he smiles, smoking his cigarette. Then he nods, stubs out his cigarette, and rises stiffly. He has a white moustache, and though the flesh of his body hangs down, he hold himself erect, in a military fashion. The woman playing patience lifts her face, but carries on playing. The boys lead him to the edge of the water. He enters the river very slowly, the water rising up his body, to the neck, to his face, he turns a little so that his eyes are visible just above the water level, looking back.

I still sit on the bench, a little detached from the scene, and then I think for a moment that he glances at me, and that the glance contains some message, some acknowledgement of my presence. If only he will just look for one moment, then he will see that I am also here, am also a part of whatever is happening.

Does he just look in my direction and not at me? He vanishes under the surface.

I stand up and walk to a point beside the two boys waiting on the bank.

The launch seems to have drifted further away.

The radio still plays on.

After some time the elder boy begins to cry out, at first teasingly, encouraging the old man to come to the surface, then with increasing concern.

The old woman gets up and stands beside us. She throws up her arms, as though dealing with tiresome children, and gestures dismissively. She lights a cigarette.

PATIENCE-PLAYING WOMAN The old fool, where is the old fool now?

22

The Great Wheel

Pleasure Garden
Morgenstadt

The Great Wheel, which can be seen from many points within the city, was constructed in 1893 as part of The International Fair held in W that year. It was designed by the Swedish engineer Brant Fisher, who also engineered the transporter bridge in Genoa and a series of rail tunnels through the Alps.
Total weight: 423 tonnes.
Diameter of the wheel: 58 metres.
Number of cabins: 17.
Rotating speed: 0.75 metres per second.
The area around the Great Wheel has been developed as a fair, with many small booths offering a variety of amusements.

The red wooden carriages hang from metal bars.

The machine, held together by slender cables, spins along a north-south line, the cars cutting across the centre of the city, up across the bowl of the sky, and then down again across the flat lands and the river. Its cycles and epicycles move within one another. From the carriages hanging at the top it might be possible to see the whole city, to assemble in one view all the separate sights.

I turn away from the wheel. Nearby lies the entrance to a mystery train. The woman sitting in the small pay-booth strictly forbids smoking, and the touching of the exhibits. I pay and sit in one of the carriages of the train. At first I think I will be alone in the train, but it is soon filled with other passengers. They squeeze in against one another and I am pushed against the side of the carriage. A whistle blows.

The train sets off into a dark tunnel, curves past tableaux illuminated by dim lights. The tableaux are arranged at various heights and on both sides so that it is impossible to take in all before the train has passed on.

OCCUPANTS OF CARRIAGE Look, look.

A heroic general stands on a mound in the woods, and speaks to his dusty troops.
Some hairy women with hairy children stand before lumpen mammoths.
A steamship, sails up a river, towards a magnificent city.
The ship's plume of smoke lies discarded on the bank.
Some natives stand on the bank, waving their arms.
A girl in a transparent box breathes heftily.

At first this decrepitude seems amusing, then I look at these things with increasing disgust. I begin to dislike this whole sentimental city, filled with these collapsing objects from its

102

past. I wonder what I could possibly hope to discover in this sequence of sights, the entire plan seems to me suddenly pointless, a way of filling in time. I reach out with my hand to push over the figures. I sense the papier mâché scraping and disintegrating against the skin of my hand. A sudden pain runs down my hand, I pull my arm back hurriedly.

The lights flicker erratically, there is darkness. The other travellers cry out. The lights shine again. There is the sound of violin music. The occupants of the carriage point with wonder at the tableaux.

OCCUPANTS OF CARRIAGE Look, look.

Magnificent horses, some with legs missing, pull a carriage, decorated with plumes and streamers and occupied by a woman and a child, through the wild mountains. Bandits appear from the trees, armed with large cutlasses. Two men kiss passionately, their arms around one another. Snow falls.

CHILD What is happening?

FATHER It must be a Christmas story. Look at the pretty trees.

SECOND CHILD The bandits are murdering the baby. Look at all the blood.

FATHER They are only playing.

The carriage is narrow, the train swings around tight corners, doubling back on itself. I am pushed against the other passengers, our arms and legs become pleasantly entangled, we leave them so.

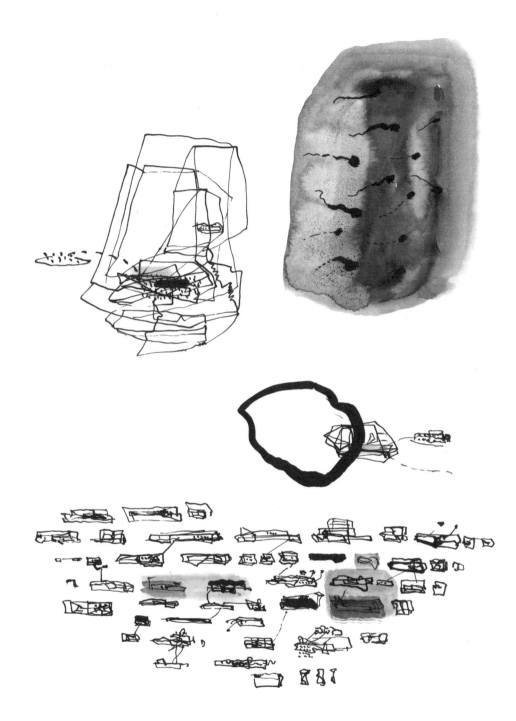

23

Tram Stop

Buenos-Aires-Gasse 37
Zernals

*The district of Zernals was originally the site of the eighteenth-
century plague pits. No sign remains now of the mass graves of
the 100,000 inhabitants of W buried here over the period 1783 –
1786. In the mid-nineteenth century, fighting between the various
immigrant nationalities took place in the area. In the 1920s a
garden city was laid out, and many villas were constructed on the
edge of the woods. The writer of crime novels, Henry Bressach,
lived on the corner of Montevideo-Gasse. He described the
area in the detective novels featuring the elegant but ruthless
investigator Monika S. Mitto. The books include –
The Episode of the Felt Hat.
The Episode of the Rheumatic Waitresses.
The Episode of the Storks Nest.
The Episode of the Meal in the Woods.
The Episode without Clues.
In Buenos-Aires-Gasse is located the tram stop with a pink steel
roof supported by rough timber columns, designed by Emil Nredda.*

A crowd of children push through into the narrow space.

Kicking and screaming and scratching, carrying a smell of unwashed flesh and stale cooking, bodies pushed up against one another, holding on to one another, arms around one another's necks, pushing away with fingers in each others faces, in each other's ears, and eyes, and noses, cutting out with elbows, pulling each other's clothes so the striped jackets and grey pullovers become distorted, pulling hair, dropping bags and packages, struggling to pick them up or kick them out of the way, legs spattered with mud, mouths grimy with spit and traces of coloured sugar, breathing hot breath into each other's faces, hating to be close to one another, but not willing to push away, all are carried along together, as one animal, not separate, not alone, tripping, falling and being picked up, calling out to each other in piping voices, the sound slipping around the hard walls, beating against the windows, not of any one voice but all together, until at last here is the door, then all push up together, squeezed even closer together through the frame of the door, into the cold air and the damp outside and so separate into small groups or some alone slipping away, still calling to each other, still jeering, wanting to be the last to be heard, still filled with the energy of having been one animal, but now allowing a sudden apartness to set in, now waiting by the tram-stop, the trams coming sharply around the corner, seeming on the point of curving from the tracks and into those waiting at the stop, then at the last moment swinging about and halting, with a screeching of metal against metal, the tramlines cutting into the ground like cruel traps for feet, try not to imagine the foot in the track, the tram wheels rolling along the tracks.

Almost evening.
The houses fading back into the shadows.

Waiting alone, no parents arriving at the stop, they must be here, no one comes and it seems late, it must be time for them to come, but maybe they forgot, that might be the car, it looks almost the same, but no another, no one to ask, perhaps they have other things to do, but surely they will send someone instead, somebody will come, the trams pass, if only somebody would come, arriving suddenly and looking worried, the other children climbing up the steps into the closed space of the tram, tired of waiting, unable to move, must wait here, must not move, but suddenly decides to climb up with the other children, not alone, pushed up amongst the others, close together, in the warmth and the stale air, the red leather seats, old women coughing, old men arguing the one with the other, the scratchy sound of the voices, holding on to the metal bar as the tram, cream white interior with pictures of mountains and lakes, bell ringing, slides away around the corners.

Afterword

It is almost always windy in W. There are three winds: the east or slow wind, the mountain wind, and the southern wind.

The slow wind blows up the valley of the Dibo out of the plains, bringing in winter clear skies and freezing temperatures, in summer hot dry days, when the temperature sometimes becomes too high for comfort, and the streets remain empty until the cool of evening time. The mountain wind, coming down from the heights to the west, brings clouds, grey days of light rain and mist, which seem to last for weeks without hope of reprieve, during which the city appears to be drained of all colour and life. The southern wind is a sign, even in winter, of warmer weather, with occasional rainy squalls, and sometimes even the smell of the sea, far to the south, pleasant periods of ease. There are also days, most frequent in autumn, when there is no wind, and a lethargic calm settles over the city, with no sign of the direction of the next wind. This period of calm has been given no name.

Index
Things Worth Seeing